STRAIGHT ASTRAY

poems by

Alessio Zanelli

TRANSFERENCE

STRAIGHT ASTRAY
Copyright © Alessio Zanelli 2005

All rights reserved. No part of this publication may be reproduced, stored in a retrieval system, or transmitted, in any form or by any means, electronic, mechanical, photocopying, recording or otherwise, without the prior permission in writing of the copyright owner.

The moral right of the author has been asserted.

Troubador Publishing Ltd.
9 De Montfort Mews
Leicester, LE1 7FW, UK
Tel: +44 116 255 9311
Email: books@troubador.co.uk

Series: Transference

Set in Palatino Linotype

ISBN 1-905237-17-0

Cover illustration:
The Night Doesn't Sleep (oil on board, 1990) by Alessio Zanelli

---

www.troubador.co.uk/transference

Straight Astray

Alessio Zanelli was born in 1963 in Cremona, northern Italy, where he still lives and works as a private financial advisor. He has long adopted English as his artistic language and has published widely in literary magazines across the world. *Straight Astray* is his third original collection in five years.

Cremona 14/10/2010

to the Editors of Chicago Review.

BY THE SAME AUTHOR

Loose Sheets
Small Press Verse & Poeticonjectures

to all those searching for their way upstream

It is difficult
to get the news from poems
yet men die miserably every day
for lack
of what is found there.

WILLIAM CARLOS WILLIAMS

Foreword

Reading Alessio Zanelli's poetry is like taking a grand and marvelous tour of sights rarely glimpsed. The setting for many of the poems in this collection is Zanelli's beloved, native Italy—though it's not the nation that most tourists happen to look for or encounter. Rather, he takes us to small towns and out-of-the-way locales, introducing us to their very human inhabitants, delving deep into their psyche and investigating their lives. It's through this exploration of people's hopes, dreams and fears that Zanelli reveals to us how much persons everywhere have in common.

Figments of love, actual nightmares, cognitive domains, remote star systems, secluded places and even mystical realms tie these verses together, as soon as the author strays far from Italy—physically or mentally—which he often does throughout the collection. Zanelli's poetry takes the reader from the deepest seas to the farthest recesses of space, from the distant past well into the future.

Zanelli's work has appeared in numerous literary journals in the United States, the United Kingdom and other countries. He uses the English language so well that it's easy to forget that it's not his mother tongue. His words fit together like the parts of a beautiful, complicated gold watch; each individual expression is precisely correct for its function but all of them work together, sweeping the reader from the beginning to the end of each poem. That said, one should not judge Zanelli's work based on the fact that he is a non-native speaker who uses the language deftly. One should instead concentrate on the fact that he is a citizen of the world and regards himself as a minute grain adrift in the immensity of an unaccountable universe.

Edgar Allan Poe once observed that a poem deserves its title when it excites the reader and elevates the soul. By traveling 'straight astray' with Alessio Zanelli, we have little choice but to be excited and have our souls elevated. These are poems in the truest sense.

DAVID LEE SUMMERS

Acknowledgments

Acknowledgments are due to the editors of the following publications, where most of these poems first appeared or are forthcoming, sometimes in slightly different versions:

Antietam Review, *Avocet*, *Bardsong*, *The Blind Man's Rainbow*, *California Quarterly*, *Comfusion*, *Concho River Review*, *Eclectica*, *First Class*, *Italian Americana*, *Main Street Rag*, *Möbius*, *The Muse Apprentice Guild*, *Poetic Voices*, *Poetry Depth Quarterly*, *Skyline Literary Magazine*, *Soul Fountain*, *Tales Of The Talisman* (formerly *Hadrosaur Tales*), *Taproot Literary Review* and *Thought Magazine* in the USA;

Aesthetica, *Dark Horizons*, *Dream Catcher*, *Editor's Choice 2003* (Poetry Now), *84's Pseudo-Chaotic Magazine*, *Exile*, *Focus*, *Harlequin*, *The Journal*, *Linkway*, *Listening To The Birth Of Crystals* (Paula Brown Publishing), *The New Cauldron*, *Orbis*, *Other Poetry*, *Pennine Ink*, *Poetry Cornwall*, *Poetry Life & Times*, *Poetry Monthly* and *Pulsar* in the UK;

Existere in Canada;

Mattoid in Australia;

Paris/Atlantic in France;

Poetry Salzburg Review in Austria.

Specially heartfelt thanks go to David Lee Summers, astronomer, writer and editor from New Mexico, whose assistance in editing this collection has proved invaluable.

Contents

Foreword	7
Acknowledgments	9
Closed Circle	15
Once Friends	16
Smooth Dancer	18
One Of The Anonymous Fallen's Lament	20
Negation	21
Drainee	22
Catharsis	23
The Reaper	25
Poet Life	26
The Pilule	27
Nocturne II	28
River Witches	29
Thrice Holy Land	30
The Pushcart	31
Phase Transition	32
Maestro	33
Rejoinees	34
Run	35
The Fax	36
The Water Snake	37
Struggling In Between	38
The Count	39
The Book	40
Menace	42
The Key	43
Equinox Reverie	44
Longing	45
Paper Heart	46
Mr. Palmer	47
The Man From The East	48
How The Night Turns Up	49
Self-Poem	50
Conjunction	52

New Year's Dictum	53
The Rush To Human Excellence	54
Seawomb	55
Invasion, Occupation, Liberation	57
A Night With You, Pablo …	59
The Unseen Hand	60
The End Has Taken Root	62
To One Who'd Want To Cross The Threshold	63
Earthbound Wait	64
Mistaken	65
The End?	66
Lowland Feel	67
Up The Hurricane's Eye	68
Lost Oneness	69
Symbionts	70
About Places	72
Mid-August Sketch	73
Sicily's Glide	74
Why There Can Be No Life On Mars	75
Sleepers	77
Solstitial Shift	78
Caution	80
Stellarcanum	81
Lone Spider	82
Cavatigozzi	83
Upside Down	84
Axiom	85
We Will Return	86
Staring At A Portrait Of Hemingway	87
In My Village	89
The Odor Of The Snow	90
First Lecture On Drunkology	92
The Dragon Has Flown	93
The Draco Prophecy	94
An Evening Clue For The Overlearned	96
Little Star	97
Frugal Supper After Her Slamming The Door	98
Year-Round Haiku	99
Guadeloupean Sunrise	102

The Long Season 103
Training 104

STRAIGHT ASTRAY

Closed Circle

Off the remotest stars,
Far beyond the barriers of space,
Way past the spheres confining obscurity,
There where time is perpetually guiltlessly late
And there's no admittance whatsoever to imperfection—
There extend huge fields of wheat and sugar beet
Intermixed with fruit tree woods and pastures,
Where countless herds uninterruptedly
Feed on strawberries and chive,
Rivers feed themselves.

There will our progeny satiate themselves,
And then so will the sons of our sons,
And so will their sons and so on.
There where our ancestors themselves
Were nourished still orphans of knowledge.

There where all of us unawares
Have drawn our being itself ever since,
Where we provided water and food out of dust,
Got light out of the dark, intrinsicality out of nihility.

And the circle will close again, then again, and whenever again.

Once Friends

How it consumes and
Meanwhile it reconciles—
The intense memory of those
Unending hours to try to shun the
Dog days, toy with locusts and
Lizards, have fun with
Blowpipes and
Fountain-jets. Of those
July Sunday afternoons—made
Of sweating and catechism, football
Kicks in the gravelly courtyard
By the church-on-hill
And psalms, to
Don the altar-boy robes
Just in time to swing the thurible
At the Benediction office. To reckon
Up time and time again the small
Coins left—to be sure to
Have enough for
One last iced pop after
The five o'clock movie. And so
That evening hide-and-seek—while
Excitedly awaiting sunset, the
Very first on-the-loose
Nightly deeds
And watches—just full
Of a whole-day-at-a-run's
Fatigue—to be late for attending
The solemn elongation of the
Moon, with tiny Venus
As her sentinel
Nearby. To be seized
With further wonder at Ursa
Major's majestic appearance, all
Of a sudden descried in the
Western sky. And now

How it consumes—
To look at ourselves in
The mirror—way inside, and
Then see all yet unchanged way up
There, all as thirty years ago
And possibly as for
Centuries of
Centuries to come. The
Slow moon and loyal Venus
Nearby, dot by dot all that twinkling
Assembly, under still-punctual
Polaris challengingly
Peering from high.

Smooth Dancer

When she danced under
my sheets—the night
seemed lynx-eyed,
hare-eared and, above
all, horse-legged.

When she blew her
cool after blowing
me—the smoke died
in my mouth without
leaving a trace.

And it was not that
bad—tossing all along
in those runaway nights,
short of breath but
with sharpened senses.

And I—sure—miss
that shivering watching,
as if having a .44's chilly
barrel pointed round the
clock against my temple.

Then she disappeared, as
always does every pleasing
dream—the night without
fail ran to sunrise quicker
than thoughts to quiescence.

A cigarette or two, the
ceiling fading away ... and
out! Some half-an-hour
sleep or just a little more,
afterwards quite a migraine.

Ultimately—each time I was
restored to daylight as a
newborn child, cheered up
by seeing my nirvana and
karma come to blows again.

One Of The Anonymous Fallen's Lament

A centurion
of the Gallic legions—
those that traversed the still-trackless Alps
in the rigors of winter,
to bring *pacem et humanitatem atque civitatem*
among the barbarian tribes of Arvernia,
to make them acquainted
with the *capitis mundi* magnificence,
then marched back home
to be saluted in triumph
on the Capitoline Hill—
one of them—I wish I had been—
rather than fight nameless battles,
in places consigned to oblivion by posterity,
under the orders of an honorless chieftain,
on behalf of a soulless home,
side by side with homeless comrades-in-arms,
because of a causeless war.
And yet in spite of my will
right that way I died—
somewhere in this tragic world,
after year 2000,
without glory nor an apology for a reason,
without benefit for anybody,
in a forgotten war
that somebody thought necessary
to the survival of the species,
or, better, to the maintenance of the *status quo*.
Aware that Nostradamus will be wrong
for who knows how many more centuries to come,
and that for me there weren't *Lares et Penates*
before whose household altar
to commend my spirit.

Negation

Man won't survive *full stop*
They've been saying that
for decades *comma*
but they'll still be there to say that
for more decades *full stop*
Man won't reach out
for other systems *comma*
they say he'll never manage
to launch manned spacecraft
beyond Jupiter's orbit *full stop*
Outliving his destiny *em dash*
man won't make it *comma*
man won't make it *full stop*
Indeed perhaps man's doomed
to the very same fate as dinosaurs' *comma*
but then someone or something else
will take over all of it *full stop*
Man's not the ultimate ruler *comma*
man's not the ultimate discoverer *comma*
man's not the ultimate unifier *full stop*
Yet who or what
all such will ever be *comma*
all that will be fulfilled in the end
still is a man's real deed *full stop* Full stop *full stop*

Drainee

She cried:
the well is dry,
the well is dry!
Bring water to the well!
And I extracted water from my body
to pour into the well,
then slept into the night.

She cried again:
the grove is ablaze,
the grove is ablaze!
Bring water to the grove!
And I extracted more water from my body
to put out the fire,
then slept into the night.

She cried once more:
the earth is athirst,
the earth is athirst!
Bring water to the earth!
And I squeezed my body to the very end
to irrigate the earth,
but could not pump so much water out of me.

So the water ran dry,
and the earth desiccated,
and she was finally silent,
and the night slept into me.

Catharsis

I—still a boy—first saw the eagle, one
of time's sly watchers, describing circles
above the spurs of Monte Disgrazia, as
the sky was shouting aloud and its savage
blue was violently blending with the unreal
white of glaciers. There and then my eyes
began to see, my ears to hear, my heart
to sift out good from evil. There and then I
began to go my own gait at a brisk and steady
pace—very long before I would meet Blake.
And I've loved to explore the *guts* of Europe ever
since—valley after valley, from the commanding
massifs of Graian and Pennine Alps, time and
again through the intimate peaks of childhood's
Rhaetian Alps, way east to the sharp but delicate
shapes of the Dolomites—for it seemed that still
so much I had to learn of time. And I sometimes
loved to caress the *thigh* of Europe as well—the
sweet and flexuous Appennine Range, from
the placid, vine-covered hills close to home
way south to momentous Vesuvio. Thereabouts
too I espied the solemn eagle on high, under
whose eye I went on with my learning of time.
But when I want to slow my pace, take my
repose, have my life back in my hands, forget
the obstinate lesson of time for a while—there's
no fitter, cozier, more easing place than the *pubes*
of Europe—the fertile, flat, alluvial piedmont plain
that saw me come into the world. Here—among
fields of maize and rows of mulberry trees, along
mighty embankments countersigned with poplars
and woody groynes that nurse the river Po—I
never happened to see the warning eagle nor
was seduced by the wiles and lures of time. Here
the gentle swallow streaks across the even gentler
sky, here I can halt a secure, relaxed, ignorant

man and have my halcyon days. And meanwhile I can ponder on the future, concentrate on the present and turn back to the past—I can embrace the infinite without unindulgent time reminding me of my dues.

The Reaper

The reaper came unseen.
It was timely though.

We heard nothing but a thud—
he couldn't say a word.

He would have said but *don't!*—
of us much more was left untold.

Poet Life

The stage is empty,
the audience—gone.
You're not aware, but
the stage is empty,
the audience—gone.
The curtain rises,
the curtain drops—
your never pull off your mask!
You ought not to deem
yourself a poet, for
other voices already told
all that must be said.
Be silent—or drop the mask!
Think it over, think again, but
hush, and hush, then hush again.
Don't waste your words,
save all your strength
to have your heart convinced of it.
The stalls and pit are desert,
your mask—I see—still on.
Be silent then, and
once and for all know
there is nothing as useless
as the word told to those
who do not want to hear.

The Pilule

He was led to believe that pilule is a minuscule sweet
to be taken each time he begins to feel blue or lonely.

Now that the drug has bored a hole in his stomach,
so many find the time to bear him company each day.

He smiles from his bed between grimaces of pain—
glad that his pilule produced in him the desired effect.

Nocturne II

As each item burns away
In a tremulous parade,
Splinters of soul—like
Red-hot brands—are
Swallowed up in the fire,
Leisurely but inexhaustible.
Its crackling scans the hours
Of the night, borrowed—if
Not robbed by fraud—from
Those of the coming day.
But a shade of sensitivity
Remains alert, just to peep
At the seminal fluid
Of the dying night streaming
Into the womb of the day.

River Witches

There beyond the main embankment,
Where silence makes itself heard
And the rook's caw suddenly bursts out
Like a crash of crumbling crystal,
There toward where inert, exhausted
Adda flows to perish into sluggish Po—
Old witches are said to have their home,
So old and crafty that the river-wind
Isn't able to catch sight of them
In the thick of riverside vegetation
Nor in the adjacent fields of Indian corn.
And they are said to revel in imitating
The far-off shouting of jubilant children,
Rather than disguising themselves
In the bark of the trees and staying
To spy on calm, unaware passers-by.
I never fear walking those places, nor
Mind the rook's trajectory, and yet
I sometimes happen to quicken my pace
Without knowing the reason why.
I don't believe there are witches
In the intertidal country, where
Horses trot and butterflies hover, and
No fisherman has ever seen one.
Still, for sure I know—had he ever
Passed down there—right there
Somewhere Van Gogh would have set
His easel, because, as he used to say
Of certain scenes, there beyond the
Main embankment, where old witches
Are said to haunt the poplar-woods and
The river-wind rarely dares to blow—
Quite the landscape goes beyond reality.

Thrice Holy Land

It's on *Time*'s cover—again!
Allah's bomb took twelve or so—
Starred tanks razed hovels to the ground.

Those bearing the Cross hold silent in between.

That way—men keep on going to the land
When on both sides there'd be need
For the land to go back to men.

The globe's rulers attend.

It's on TV right now—again!
This time the bomb took only ten—
Soon will endangered David take revenge.

The Pushcart

It's got brighter colors now
than it had about thirty years
ago—when old Cilia's wrinkly
hands pushed it to the stairway
to the church, any given Sunday
afternoon. No more chestnuts
roast and crackle on it, no more
chick-peas peep—no more candy
nor peanuts. Now younger hands
embellish it with every sort of
flower by the florist's shop, it
no longer runs the comical risk of
slipping out of Cilia's hold down
the village alley. Now it's always
lustrous and fragrant—let aside in
a shady corner but in perfect order
as it had never been when carrying
seasonal tidbits for jubilant kids.

Phase Transition

From October through March homeland borrows
its breath from the river. For days the fog
becomes the sole thing that can be seen. When
it paralyzes the country, streets, trees
and houses vanish, shapes and contours change,
each man's or nature's work doesn't exist. When
it saturates the space, the sky sublimes,
sounds are muffled, the air smells. Everything
undergoes a phase transition, fuses
into the sole thing—the fog. Londoners
and those who mythicize the fumes of the
city would panic at it, if driving
through, would stop and leave their cars, go on on
foot off the road. We—residents of the
place—always find our way home; it is our
land. Such fog has bred us up, has filled our
lungs and wet our eyes from birth, and still will
condense to droplets or rime upon our
abodes to come. We know it; we can trace
and put each thing back to its place inside
it just because of our blood and our noses.

Maestro

A dish of soup, a piece of cheese, two
glasses of wine. In exchange for a
painting. That way he bartered life—he
seldom paid for a meal. He taught us
to see, hear, understand—he taught us
to draw lines and circles, use colors,
depict our lives. Essay on Mondays,
math on Wednesdays, general culture
on Saturdays. Visiting farms and
factories in autumn and museums
in winter, outdoor learning in spring—
in such a manner we spent our
prime years. So many in our town still
remember his tobacco-yellowed
mustache, his cavalryman attire
and gentleman's demeanor. As a
youth he'd had a hand in making the
tunnel of Eiger-Mönch-Jungfrau, fired
some rifle-shots in World War II and
took a Red Cross nurse as his wife
thro' correspondence. He was just *the*
schoolmaster and it mattered little
if sometimes he liked to have a
drop too much and smoked without
respite. He used to say he was of Jewish
descent and believed in God, his way,
always told us we could abnegate
anything save being ourselves to the
end. Not everyone held him in
esteem—many mocked him because
of his hair and style, others envied
him in silence. Not everyone
loved him, nevertheless we still do—
we know he's been our only Maestro.

Rejoinees

We ran our childhood wild together as
rebellious, teasing little rascals, spent
a dozen winters under common roofs—
as many summers over common yards.

Then came the day our palship living took
to wane until it seemed to be gone-by—
our twosome gang disbanded then, although
indeed the thread has never broken since.

Now that our roads have come across again—
with in between his seven years alone
in the Peruvian Andes caring for
the poorest and mine as many passed to advise

the richest how to grow much richer—I
would like our trades to turn to one awhile.
I wish we could retrieve a bit of that
of us we have discarded through the past,

resume some common habits, drink a toast
on what we were, we are, we'll be. Just talk,
forgive each other's having walked apart—
perhaps write down four-handed poems anew.

Run

Run forward, run as long and far as legs can reach—
but see the sun and clouds float still ahead of you.

Run forward, run as tight and fast as lungs can stand—
again you have the sky and all within precede.

Then keep in view you'll have to stop, retrace your
 steps—
the sky's allowed to drift along and glide away.

The Fax

The Fax, so hard to explain. Pictures are fading as well. That time, at the cottage near the confluence of the two rivers in flood, there were the chiefs and a few others. Driving rain for days had reduced the whole site to a bog. The King was on vacation. Inside there were laughter and shouting, empties collecting on the tables, the air and everything saturate in smoke. Joe, one of the seniors, had bet that Geo, one of the juniors, could make it quite well. Some others had their little money on him. Paio, another senior, had bet his underpants against the feat. Of course he lost. Geo gulped down—pat after pat—five kilos of cold polenta, drowning it in his stomach with nearly as many liters of barbera. The most impressive thing was that he made it in no more than two hours. The remainder of the night was not that memorable. Most of those present eventually flopped down asleep, only a few stayed awake till dawn to mutter nonsense away, from cig to cig, sipping never-final stirrup-cups and looking at Geo's eyeballs swelling up but twinkling in the shade. A pale, reddish sun filtered through the morning mist on the horizon, the water by then was lapping at the gate and the improvised parking lot. They left higgledy-piggledy, as they were used to doing, by run-down cars or bikes. Today most of them are married, have a child or two, some more dead cells in their brains, a little less alcohol in their veins, fewer excesses on their minds, many dreams gone-by. Somebody has even somewhat made his way. And yet somebody sometimes comes to the fore again, just for fun, no more for the records. They meet twice or thrice a year, each time some more are missing the roll-call. Nonetheless the story goes on, with quite a bunker-manor, a larder-cellar-court, a *chef de marmites et poêles* Monarch ... till when ... who knows?

The Water Snake

Irregularly fashioned fields of sunflowers, corn and
soybean—a plotless tapestry discontinuously
    intagliated
among the suburban domains. At a run, on
    occasion
accompanied by cautious ravens and snooping
    stray dogs.
Sporadically sighting hares and pheasants, some
swallows, rare herons. Still, the most unlikely
    encounter
today is that with the water snake—the green or
the dark-gray one—by surviving ponds and
    runnels.
And think that once it hissed between my feet—
slipping through miraculously untrod!
But it no longer is the age of rural quiet—the time
and place for little, lonely farmsteads.
Hard times for packing hay or reaping crops.
Hard times for the cross-country runner.
Hard times for the water snake.
It no longer is the time for all that foots or crawls
    across the land.

Struggling In Between

He wants to hang paintings on the moon,
have the ocean listen to him and discover
how to turn to an immense Swarowski.

He wants water and fire to be good friends,
flora and fauna to converse with men,
fog, rain, hail, rhyme and snow to decorate his
    home.

He wants to silence quacks and frauds,
have those who stand in silence talk
to tell us all the truth about our faked world.

He wants the universe to be unique, a holistic plot
to unfold inside his mind, a manifold unity
to disclose outside by means of his words and
    deeds.

He fails to recall the initial extreme he started from
and barely remembers some tracts of his way,
but now feels clearly the final extreme
    approaching.

He does not have a magic wand nor supernatural
    powers,
he is just a man halfway between the extremes
on a desperate essay to leave an evidence.

The Count

I'm the only Count in town
he used to grumble
in his cups,

leaning on *Il Conte*'s walls—
the village tavern
named like him.

I'm a skunk like no one else,
I'm made as five plus
five makes ten.

He kept loyal to himself,
observed his precepts
till the end.

So cirrhosis sent the bill
amid his sixties—
he paid toll.

He was not even left time
to think and choose a
worthy heir.

And although so many indeed
could claim his title,
no one will.

No other wino crawls in
the streets to jabber
I'm the Count.

Water didn't suit him, but—
be sure—he hasn't
passed athirst.

The Book

I know what it's doing to you, even though
I don't know why. I see you close the door
when, sitting alone in the room, you bend
over the book, immerse yourself thoroughly
in it, to reemerge only at the agony of night
with the marker ever closer to the end.

It absorbs all of your energies, affects all of
your molecules—all that you are and will be,
even your shadow. You might just lock the
door and escape my eyes, but what you ought
to fear remains inside. You're safe from me,
but not from what in it inexorably devours you.

Like the exorcist the breviary, like the exegete
the Bible, you stare at the open book without
reading it, as if you knew everything by heart.
It will lead you—without your realizing it or
being able to avoid it—where you would never
go, nor will I ever be able to prevent all this.

I can't intervene from outside, nor help you in
any other way. Only closing the book or taking
it away from under your eyes would do. That
door is blocking me, not its pages in the least.
I can hear you turn them circumspectly, one
after another, I can even hear you breathe it in.

I can see what hunts you, I know what haunts
the book. Soon you'll no longer be able to close
it yourself. I foresee what will then happen to
you, even though I don't know why. I'd want to
shake and wake you, but I can't. If you only
knew what has you—how true and bad it is.

You and those blank pages—that book consumed
with dust without one letter typed in it. You and
the nothingness you read in it for endless nights
will soon be one—forever. I know this from your
silence and sighs, from your sacred thumbing of
the pages. I do know all this, but I don't know why.

Menace

The professionals of time
weren't able to defuse the device—
it can be read on their faces,
horror—on anybody else's face.
The ticktock continues,
disregarded but inexorable.
None will be spared by the terrific blast—
everything will be lost in a second.
All that can be touched,
all that can be thought—
swept away.
Millenary traditions so far preserved,
the footsteps of those who preceded—
erased.
The crucial attainment,
the basing condition,
the awareness of ruling race—
annihilated.
What will be left
is the absolute vacuum
of a novel, amnesic beginning.
Time is to fill the void
and enable another headway,
but—perhaps—not to mankind.

The Key

lost in her microcosm
in search of flares
in which to burn
for eternity

        inattentive seeker
        jaundice-blind observer
        of ordinary bodies

                unaware of trapping
                in his focus
                the nova of a lifetime

        the end of the quest
        for a private door on her
        the key to her world

like quarks
baryon-confined
inseparable instants
glued together in love

Equinox Reverie

musing
at golden-bordered
cotton layers
drifting in the blue
forward on my route

> late sunbeams
> like red-hot razor-blades
> cut through my pupils

but I'm already blind

> blind to the light
> as deaf to the sound
> and callous to the touch
> that be not those
> from my unhealable self

a minute cloud
solitarily fraying away
in September clear but crowded sky

> how restful to intuit

eyes beyond the visible
watch over and retain

> not a single particle down here
> is to remain unrecorded

Longing

lights saturate

        gather and merge
        as into a hole

moments later
the disc drops below

        from there the dusk
        arises

out there the evening
stands against the glow

        the mute land slips away
        suffused with the slow transition

absconded spectators long to be espied

Paper Heart

tight grasp
sharp words
are all you used
no hit no flame

cold blade
in the flesh
without bones
without blood

cold breath
so dense
so weighty
in too hot air

deep tear
among whispers
and farewell rustles
of a balled heart

don't pick it up
it won't unfold
don't even try
just let it roll

Mr. Palmer

Mr. Palmer gathered wood
and resold it just to keep
the pot boiling—sometimes
had the luck to gather
even iron and copper.
When not engaged with the bottle,
he also liked to incise wood.
He carved—at times inlaid—walnut,
briar, oak, mahogany and cherry,
if only someone brought him some.
He skillfully handled
chisels and gouges—
when able to retrieve them.
He used to carve pieces of art
for next to nothing or a cig,
just as an opponent artist's
tools—the smoke and wine indeed
he never ceased to love so much—
inchmeal furrowed his face, stomach
and lungs till demise.
Mr. Palmer ultimately let cancer make
himself his acknowledged masterpiece.

The Man From The East

I have no carry-on luggage,
no documents, no identification marks,
no photographs, no good-luck pieces—
nothing that could say who I am.
My story is blowing in the wind,
in the gelid blast from the continental waste
where nothing else than flat land can be seen.
No matter who I am, what I may tell—
the wrinkles on my forehead speak for me,
so do the angularity of my features
and the roughness of my hands.
Above all speaks the gloss in my eyes,
unceasingly turned to the distance.
Don't investigate my identity,
the place I come from and those I quit,
the whys and wherefores.
Suffice it to say where I'm bound—
at a slow but steady pace,
a little crooked but head erect.
I chase my destiny westward,
further west I will only stop.
The greatest sea awaits me agog—
there at the end of the land,
where my walk will be over,
the wind pushing me will subside,
a new contrary one will rise.
Listen to the blast from the East,
my voice: who I was, I am, I will be—
blowing from where I will go nevermore.
That wind—my life,
that land—my journey,
that sea—my dream.
The dust that blast will finally drop—
my only personal belongings,
my only legacy indeed.

How The Night Turns Up

Emerald eyes, raven
curls and scarlet attire
is how the night appeared
last time. I wanted hazel,
blonde and nude—in that
order—though. I'd told
you that—it's you who
don't believe the night is
never pleasing me. I'll
remonstrate with the
dreammaker, I'll show
you how to plead! I'll give
her one more chance, and
if she still doesn't want
to comply with my lust—
I'll replace her with
some easier fancy. And
you! Abstain from laugh
and scoff, since I quite
know the way you try to
have her pop in and strip
off slow. I'm not jealous,
but as to rebuking friends—
unhesitatingly zealous.

Self-Poem

Here's the bond—what
ties though seems to insert
abysmal distances—the
overall case, the philosopher's
stone, the missing link, the
ultimate element.

Proceeding from quantum
resonances not less than from
vers libre. Offspring of both
scientists and scholars—laws
and lines converge, the two
descriptive systems merge.

Rubbia and Luzi will
applaud, so would Planck
and Rilke, and way back to
Newton and Pope. Progeny
of pioneers of matter and
word—man's now close.

The thorough unifier—what
doesn't demand any further
definition. From poetry to
science and from science to
poetry. The circle's being
squared, the voyage's over.

Transient in body, fixed in
time. Eternauts—we're now
fully cognizant, we now can
see. Simplicity and completion
and self-inference. Jason and
Orpheus, Urania and Euterpe.

Let Charon be done with his
task, man with his quiz, God
with His plan. Afresh—the
boson of Higgs, the perfect
lines. Now the universe has
its own fingers, ears and eyes.

Conjunction

Sidereal-footed
dancing,
reeling led
by spiral arms.

Nova-eyed
and pulsar-hearted,
grasping at a blow
and no more querying.

The infinitely small
enfolding
the infinitely big,
beauty embedded within.

Crossing the barrier,
zigzagging nebulae and
wormholes throughout,
each other embraced.

God's face bared
by means of a kiss
as a smile is pictured
on the lips of the world.

New Year's Dictum

An adage has that what
one does upon the new

year's day is what it will
be mostly doing through all

the year. If that's the case
then quite long sleeps, a bit

of writing teamed up with
rash drinking wait for me.

The Rush To Human Excellence

From mankind's dawn to dusk, through
magnificent cultures of ancient Egypt,
China, Mesopotamia, the Maya, the Celts,
the Urnfield people, Greece, Persia, Rome,
and on up to present-day alleged postwar
global civilization—each one exhibits
its own aberrations, barbarisms, excesses,
whereby one trait is always handed down
unchanged: the thunderous call for victims.
None is known to have not claimed a huge
death toll. From the savagely-slain to the
left-slowly-agonizing ones, whenever and
wherever, with clamor and emphasis as in
silence and out of sight—one cry. And the
killed ones augment at a faster rate than
the spared ones—such is the unpreventable
cost of *human progress*. To each culture its
kinds of slavery, its horrors, its apartheids,
its pogroms, as to the extent of which our
space age really shines unprecedented.

Seawomb

When they gave me
my first and only
navigational instruments,
I didn't believe
they meant business
and I really was
to steer the ship
and plot my course.

As I thought
it had happened
to Magellan, Cook,
Amundsen or any other
past explorer searching
for their fate—that we kids
may pore over in a book—
so I expected
it was the *good course*
that would find *me*,
then out of harm's way
lead me from haven to haven.

That's why
I never plied the sextant,
paid attention to the winds,
took and managed the helm.

Oh, false presumption!

How difficult—now—
to chart a course,
follow its line asea
and carry the fear along,
like Columbus had to quell
discontent, revolt, despair.

How to sail
much too vast and deep a sea?

The course I trace in it
is never mine;
I feel enmeshed
in a blue whale's baleen,
but I'm not as lucky
as Jonah was ...
who at least couldn't see
where he was forced to go.

Let me chance on you—*terra firma*,
take and keep me someway,
deplete my hold
and quench my drifting fever.

I never was a sailor,
nor a castaway, however;
I'm just a wavy foetus
at the mercy of a seawomb
from which I'm never born.

Invasion, Occupation, Liberation

        Invaded—

held tightly
    by the shoulders,
        pulled fiercely
            by the hair.

She felt
    the flesh into the flesh,

screamed and struggled,
then hushed and kind of thought

        she was going to die.

She bore inside
    what she believed a fiend,
became a corpse that housed
some stranger life—

        a sort of evil occupier.

She finally expelled it,
    feeling freed at once
from all of her horrible burdens—

        the baby

screamed and struggled,
then hushed and kind of thought

        it was going to live.

    She looked at it and took it in her arms—

        revived.

That beautiful child
is now the whole of her life—

    her liberation in the flesh.

A Night With You, Pablo …

A night with you, Pablo, brooding
on the plots of time, the warpings of
the soul in order to second the body, the
grooves in which days run, life moves.

Ah, Pablo … how shrewd, how brisk, how
pert you were; but plain, and straight, and
sage, and quiet … *A Pesar de la Ira*.

What a fearless, fearful singer; extoller
of love and hate, detractor of elation and
dejection, master of felicity and sorrow.

How much godhead in your mundane
speaking … *La Palabra*; how much spirit
in your flesh … *Cuerpo de Mujer*.

You always knew … *El Desconocido*, I
just begin to; ah, Pablo … *No Hay Olvido*.

I won't! I won't! *Oh Tierra, Espérame*.

Too short, the night.
Too strong, the light.

Where is it I got lost, Pablo?
Whatever odyssey is this?

Eyeless, my hand.
Handless, my eye.
Eager, my mouth.
Too short, the night.

Ah … *La Soledad*!

Nothing is worth my suppliant words.

The Unseen Hand

I warn you not to be ordinary, I warn you not to be young,
I warn you not to fall ill, and I warn you not to grow old.

NEIL KINNOCK

I'm not afraid of playing
with hazards, secrets, jams, taboos;
shame and fear in others' eye
become aplomb and spunk in mine.
I sneer at habits, tenets, canons,
fashions, charges, stereotypes;
at that ubiquitous pattern
in which each man attempts to keep afloat
but often ends by drowning.
I shrink from all that's standardized
though claims the contrary;
from etiquettes, clichés, musts:
the latest model of luxury SUV,
a set of exclusive stylist suits,
a most rapid, brilliant career,
a lovely, tailored wife that always cheers.
Bingo!
I know who you are,
beneath what guise you hide,
behind what status symbol;
I know where your panicking ego
is used to fleeing and seeking refuge;
you who cut my way
and feel your members shake,
your heartbeat quicken,
your visage redden.
I haven't arrived at all costs;
I haven't grown either rich
or famous or anyway special.
I'm not unscratchable by events
nor refractory to sorrow;
I'm definitely aging,
I'm not running after time

and I know I'm eventually going to die.
All I have is myself
and somebody to love, requited;
somebody with whom to desire
to be happy indeed.
Nothing else, nothing else at all,
nothing of all that you're used to airing.
But I can withstand your look,
keep mine fixed until you lower yours.
And whatever hand you may hold,
should we ever sit face to face,
I can lay my cards on the table,
absolutely sure that you
will have already closed your eyes
and renounced the kitty.

The End Has Taken Root

The time has come—

>of the black on the blue,
>of flares, of gales, of dusts;
>of quick pandemonium
>and then perennial calm.

>>Of no return.

The time has come—

>forever, now,
>to see stars burst and fall;
>we watch, we hear,
>we wait to disappear.

>>We must be gone.

The time has come—

>at last a vainly spinning mottled sphere
>nobody ever will descry;
>residual waves adrift in empty space
>nobody ever will detect.

>>Unpicked-up echoes of late throes.

To One Who'd Want To Cross The Threshold

Quiet. Be quiet or die. Let others
go—obliged. Withdraw your step and
stop, restrain your hand, return your
stare. Be quiet and look then fancy

your imago past the threshold,
but don't make a move! That's not a
task of yours, the where and how and
when. Whatever your intention

is—your creed or your desire—just
see what has you live and know that
you must die before you're made to
know. That's how it goes, how Someone

gives and takes away, how governs
and continually creates. Be
quiet, be on your own, and hush, and
learn, and wait. There's time—this I can

state right now—on either side of
such alleged divide. So much, and
quite the same, indeed. Yet there can
be no prescience, gauge or figure.

Earthbound Wait

I hold that the characteristic of the present age is craving credulity.

BENJAMIN DISRAELI

And he remains on his own
looking upwards, as if some
heavenly conveyance should
appear then alight and call
to pick him up, to rescue
him from the dissipations
of mundane living. And he
surely believes this world not
to belong to him, or the
other way around, expects
that everything will be soon
uncovered. And he waits, waits
confidently, sigh after
sigh, heaping smiles and gazes
full of sympathy. As if
he were the only one to
know, the end of his wait just
minutes away. With upturned
face and darting eyes, never
tired of healing his bruises
nor of trying to avoid the
blows dealt by time all the time.

Mistaken

They spend their time mostly looking forward to the past.

JOHN OSBORNE

I know I was mistaken, but—
don't even try to wrong my past.

Okay—we used to come to blows
or kicks, to pelt each other wild

with stones, to clash from morn to eve
on every given day of those

unending summer months we spent
as lads defiled with earth and sweat.

I know I was mistaken, but—
don't even try to foul my name.

Because your town's remained as small
as mine, your puerile dreams have flawed

like mine, your careless push has waned
to easier poise like mine, the world

in which we find ourselves is not
the one we both had meant to be.

I know I was mistaken, but—
that is the past—just yours like mine.

The End?

I'm bound to sink
to look for light.

Much time to think,
no time to write.

Too glum to weep—
I drop my eyes.

The cut runs deep—
no truths, no lies.

Lowland Feel

They say the sun describes
the final tract of its diurnal arc
more quickly,
while sunset is the most solemn instant
of the day—kind of perceived
as a noetic terminator
that separates physical existence into units.
What a real pity
that here in the alluvial plains
such spectacle can be viewed only rarely,
since the evening brume
is used to thickening before the disc,
making it dissolve
when still above the horizon to a degree.
And maybe it's just because of this
that we in the lowlands
never mind the times of the sun,
not even when it stays away for days or weeks.
It is fixed and immutable in our perspective—
as it is in space in truth—
although it appears
to be eternally moving in its trajectory.
We are accustomed to its casual presence,
don't notice its twilight race to nocturnal hiding
and know it's always there,
albeit disguised by undispellable fog.
Motherland didn't provide us
with receptors apt to contemplate
single, momentous, unforgettable events.
She rather shaped our minds and bodies
so as to last through a thorough life
exclusively made
of consecutive, everyday, fugitive instants.

Up The Hurricane's Eye

What a strain,
what an indescribable thrill—
feeling on the verge
of being inescapably swept away.

Love, hate, joy, sorrow—
no experience might compare
with as terrible a proof.

I'm not afraid that I may lose myself,
I'm not afraid that you may lose yourself.

It's coming—
punctual, inexorable;
puerilely mindless of its power.
Blind but accurate.

The second that embraces
the whole of our existence.

And it's not for fear
that all we are now might soon be over—
I fear nothing but our being smashed apart:
you and me—torn and screaming
on opposite sides of nowhere.

Nothing else scares me—
not life, not death!

So hug me tightly,
hold on to me all out;
and once flung away,
but still one thing—
may the hurricane's eye inbreathe us on high.

Lost Oneness

Our country is the world—our countrymen are all mankind.

                    WILLIAM LLOYD GARRISON

From antipodean worlds, from disjointed milieux,
from reciprocal enclaves—one mankind
proceeds, multiplies, expires.

One but riven, severed into vestigial splinters
sickly dragging along, in their finity's affinity.

Myriads of trails—originated from distant cradles
but forever impressed on the only surface—converge
to the only precipice, on the verge of the only deep.

The common stare—nonplussed—contemplates
the sweep below, inundating the horizon
as far as the eye can reach.

And from the sinking light a domineering recall arises,
then turns to regret, in the end to ache for the wasted
    time.

Along with shades, the early inducement returns
ever stronger each night—the idea of diving into that sea.

Closing the eyes, waiting a long while
then traversing the expanse on the instant,
sensing at last what teems in the mind
of the neighbor opposite the world.

Becoming one again.

Symbionts

       You—

who know who I am, inside as well outside, of
which game I am a pawn, what makes me amble
as it likes, like a somnambule, what maneuvers
me by means of invisible threads—

       you—

            be
            my foot,
            my hand,
            my mouth.

       You—

who can spot where every wobbly, erratic
step of mine alights, envision where the next
one is likely to fall, make your own way, act
and speak of your own accord—

       you—

            be
            my spoor,
            my tirade,
            my invective.

       You—

who can penetrate all this, as in perfect
symbiosis, throughout aware—

       be
       me,
       just me,
       all me.

  You—

make no scruple, drain my life-force and
burn away my whole caged anger—

         if you can't really cut those threads.

About Places

So many are the places that I've seen,
at first on books, a student, then on site,
a tourist; either works of nature or

of man: Hardanger Fjord, Grand Canyon, then
Stonehenge, the ruins of Rome. And even more
are those I'd love to visit still: the South Pole,

the Great Barrier Reef, then Troy, the Valley of
the Kings. I know I'll get to view but few
of all such places; too, what out of all

my doubts is mainly gnawing in my brain
is where it is I'll have to go, to which
resort I'll be appointed in the end.

I'll fly to Zion or cross the river Styx?
Of Gods, if blessed, which pantheon shall I see?
Of Dante's rings, if damned, which shall claim me?

Mid-August Sketch

          She drained
the last inch of her negroni
only when the sun was culminating,
          stood up
without uttering a word and
          made off
zigzagging apace through the noontide heat,
swaying her hips down the crowded *piazza*—
          leaving me with
one last bill,
a couple of used straws
and three dripping rocks to suck.

          I turned
my eyes to the dial
of the renaissance belfry's clock,
          stared
at the imperceptible movement of its hands,
not at the hour indicated,
          musing
on her reptile heart and
          mutely jeering
at my gander brain.

          I then upped
in like manner,
to shake off sultriness,
and all of a sudden
          felt
some fifty looks attached to me,
          as if I wore
one of those ludicrous,
four-coned, multicolored Lappish headgears—
          I stepped.

Sicily's Glide

Like jets of lava from revived Etna your disgorgements
of hate are bruising me. Fierce, incandescent,
   unremitting.
But what scares me is not being hit by your lapilli, I'm
accustomed to cope with such uninhibited eruptions.
   What
really terrifies me is your love's subterranean recoil to the
bottom of the fault. And that tremulous flame, yet
   smoldering
under the thick blanket of ashes. I know what the
   volcano still
keeps in store for me and I'd better put to sea, sail off the
nuée ardente, head due northeast, coast through the Strait
of Messina and be willing to face both Scylla and
   Charybdis.

Why There Can Be No Life On Mars

She said she'd never comply
with his request; she'd rather run
the New York marathon
or climb K2 on her own.
She restated she'd never, ever
do that, anyway;
then added that she maybe would,
if little green men
should actually land, and make her.

He took exception to her resolve;
indeed, he flew off the handle
and began to curse her,
shouting as if he were possessed.
She swore at him with equal vehemence,
even while she completed her toilette.

They went on like that
throughout the damned night,
watching *The Thing From Another World*
for the hundredth time,
sprawled out apart on the couch,
sipping beer and crunching popcorn
without restraint,
exchanging scowls from time to time.

That's why brewers, maize growers
and TV makers will never go broke,
safe as attorneys and morticians.
This also explains why there can be no life on Mars.

NASA'd better take it into account
and revise its space program.
UFO fans ought to understand, ought to put an end
to the laughable pretense we're not alone.

So, gulp down beer and popcorn at your ease
while watching the twentieth repeat of *Star Trek*,
and don't forget to cast the evil eye at your spouse.
Above all, keep on making
indecent requests of each other.
I have just purchased professional-quality ear plugs.

Sleepers

Surviving.
Clinging to grimaces
that never turn to smiles.
Outliving the present.
Outliving the absence of time.
Gulping days in sequence,
while seconds gulp us at one go.
Waiting for someone
to pull us out from dream.
Waiting.
As if hoping
that an icy bubble
might seal us up inside.
Making everything
our endless night.
Believing it is hers
the smile escaping us.
Pretending
we belong to her forever.
But the morning comes on the dot.
And we're regularly late.
And we can't stand the glow.
And we're unable to speak.
To stay as well as to quit.
That's it.

Solstitial Shift

Ring … snooze … ring … stop!
5:10 a.m.—the coppery dawn
like an electroshock.

Through the window
fragrance of grass just mown,
afloat in the liquid air,
prompting to up and stir.
Teasing ghosts in the dark rooms
hindering each move,
even no time to switch on the light—
the gold-turning glow will do.

Clothes, papers, car key—
everything OK for the journey.
A last glance at the baggage
plus a quick toothbrushing.
No breakfast, of course,
but a hasty snack of the heart:
grandpas and uncles sensed
to be amazedly watching
from the bookcase shelves.
I'll be back—I swear it!

I'll fly back along with cranes,
when merry dancers take to shine.

Eastward the sky is pure fire;
now the air is soaked
in each substance or spirit
rising from homeland earth.
All is apparent silence still;
all is but paradoxical thrill.

And now the stranger is me.

He goes up the ramp
anticipating those epic dawns
in the furthermost North—
only made of patinated silver,
soporific smells, soothing elves
and absolute pillow-sinking.

Caution

This is not a poem.

Whatever you may think—
it isn't.

Whoever happens
to read these lines
must abstain from thinking
they're reading a poem.

Rather,
they must abstain from thinking anything.

More,
they mustn't read these lines at all.

Don't read these lines—
they hardly make a poem.

And should you want to read them regardless,
rest assured you'll be never considered a poetry reader.

This is not a poem.

Stellarcanum

Stars scribble on our eyes the frosty sagas,
The gleaming cantos of unvanquished space.

                      HART CRANE

You—
unsoundable body
falsely adrift in unsoundable space.
Let me chart the vacuum you move in,
calculate your trajectory,
analyze your spectrum.

You—
once predictable star
along the main sequence.
Now I can see you glistening away,
finally reborn binary,
closely remote.

Now capture me,
me—
novel David Bowman urged astray.
Just pull me up and sling me forcibly
into a sighting orbit eternally entwined
around your mysterious twin spheres.

Or seal me out forever blind.

Lone Spider

Me and non-me,
home and afield,
life and departure,
everything and its opposite.

These words are my only offspring,
these marks—the precepts and teachings I impart to
    them.

These words and marks
are the reason why I'm used to being alone,
to laboring and musing on my own.

Like a menhir in a one-menhir circle.
Like a galaxy in a one-galaxy universe.

These words are my atoms and stars,
these marks—my links and radiations.

And why I don't care to continue in someone else.

Like a lone spider in a dark garret,
only intent on spinning its web.

My web of words and images,
of marks and patterns—
the scheme, the representation, myself.

Words—just words within words.
Fixed, obsessive words.
And mobile, relieving marks.

What they make altogether anew is the spider I am—
and the fierce, desperate loop never ends.

Cavatigozzi

What would you think or do
should you live in a place called *Cavatigozzi*?

Kah-vah-tee-goh-tzee.
You'll never have me articulate its name again!

Even the village doesn't know.
I too live there and am at a loss for words.

Just take the place, the name, the people as they are—
take life over there as it comes day by day.

Upside Down

What sort of world is ever that
where order and peace are made through soldiers
and tumult and war are made through pacifists?

Axiom

Man's wickedness is the price to be paid
for the self-cognizance of the universe.

We Will Return

It is as though the words of that instant
had been transparently incised
on the glass screening the photograph.

We will return as alien brothers,
and we will realize our common roots
from the daydreams flashing in our eyes
and the hectic motions of our hands.

Alien—sure—after long diverging,
but we will return at the proper time
to stamp on the very same slice of soil.

When our common sky gets low
and the space below gets thin;
when the brash and teasing clouds
of the unending summer
stretch out like azure blades
in the twilight blue to north
above the outline of the Alps.

We will return as ancient brothers,
soon forgetful of our respective roads just left,
and there will be no sky that may still crush us.

Just words from a mutely-spying photograph,
words full of promise—so far unkept—
and the obstinate summer now long gone.

Staring At A Portrait Of Hemingway

Each of us—
and the illusion of ruling
what instead possesses us
since we were conceived.

Each of us—
and the whole containing us
as well as contained in us,
receptacles of each other.

Some cosmic link disturbs
and soothes us at one time,
without our being aware.
Each of us and all the others!

Like the old man and the sea—
unwrinkled the one, waveless the other;
naïvely trusting to have escaped
the infallible sculptor's chisel.

Each of us—
and all of us.
Sharing the insolent fate of being alone
and all one at the very same time.

Like the old man and the sea—
the one the unaware cause of the other;
each oblivious of the other
though closely facing for eternity.

The old man—each of us,
intent on ogling the sea—all of us,
the image of what he would have been,
before the sea disperses it forever.

Ernest always knew—
his eyes speak from the glossy paper.
Each of us—
hence none of us.

In My Village

In my village
men no longer have
lips to smile,
just to roar with laughter;
women no longer have
eyes to weep,
just to swell with unshed tears.

In my village
boys don't know what to make
of streets, nights, books and girls;
girls don't love
to talk, play, dream and be loved.

In my village
three thousand trucks each day
overdose the air with tar particulate;
the wind rarely blows,
the snow deserts.

In my village
nothing's realized anymore,
not the days, not the sky, not the people;
even the fog appears to be gone,
along with spring, fall and babies.
Life splashes about like a tadpole
in an ever-smaller puddle.

The Odor Of The Snow

A gull gliding overhead—
        parrying the icy flakes
        or letting them slide
        off the silver plumage,
        solitary and somewhat disoriented
        yet always vigilant
        and assiduously shifting
        in perfect circles—
will ever wonder
the reason why below
one man is running—
        so fiery and resolute,
        as if bound for a faraway
        but certain destination—
through and against the driving graupel?

Neither knows
that what draws both of them
in the open country—
        each one by its own peculiar kind of motion,
        route and degree of awareness—
is the very same hunting game,
the same scornful trick of the dying season.
Or of the dawning one?

It's the same primordial need
of something indefinite—
        some call it freedom,
        some call it affirmation of the self—
which possesses every living being from birth
and sets it going forever.

It's at bottom the same insuppressible instinct—
        tracing back to remote ice ages—
that drives both of them.
The one to trail

and eventually deeply inhale
the odor of the snow,
on the continuous effort
to accomplish their part—
         minimal but requisite—
in the gigantic plot by an invisible hand.

It's just the odor of the snow.

First Lecture On Drunkology

How curious to note
how drunks look identical
and act in the very same way
everywhere in the world.
Each place has personages of its own—
its politicians, its trendsetters, its highbrows,
its demagogues, its execrators, its snobs, and so on.
But drunks are the same in all places,
whoever they are or whatever they do when sober.
Even more remarkably and particularly—
drunkards have the same face,
the same tongue, the same stench,
the same anything, wherever they are.
Definitely and finally—
they all share one nationality.

The Dragon Has Flown

Now droops
The arm—the
Taut muscle
Relaxes. The
Step draws
Back as the
Eyes gaze at
The flattened
Expanse of the
Sea. Everything
Bursts with
Quiet—gone is
The lividity of
Yore. Died
Down—the
Force of the
Tempest. All—
Intent upon
Milder affairs.
Relented—he
Who used to
Yell. And once
For all the
Dragon has flown.

The Draco Prophecy

Among all forms of mistake, prophecy is the most gratuitous.

GEORGE ELIOT

They said he would ride the aurora borealis,
tame the fury of maddened oceans,
make the midday sun pale
by simply pointing a finger to the zenith.
They said he could do without anything and anybody
whereas nothing and nobody could do without him;
they would grow weary of counting
the days of his unchallenged dominance,
his dawns as the chieftain of the just
and his dusks as the victor of the abject.
Nothing could ever shake the yoke
he would superimpose on the great rebel—time.
Nobody could ever tell him what to do,
when to speak or where to go.
He could freely do anything he wanted
but would never be forced to do anything he didn't.

This, and much more, they said.

He overstepped the unmarked limit
without their noticing him, in perfect silence,
on a rare night stolen from the still-young spring
by the overpowering and brazen winter.
He still hadn't learned to hold the reins
nor seen nor done anything of what they'd predicted.
Yet it can't be said if the prophecy
has really turned out to be false,
since they never stated if they referred to before or after.
And he thus went away, unseen, on the wings of Draco,
while it wound its coils round the Little Bear to north.
When the coda of biting southing winds
divested peaches, plums and cherries
of their short-lived gaudy vestments.
Like a dream long dreamed not knowing it's a dream.

Indeed he now shines in the eye of Draco.

An Evening Clue For The Overlearned

Stars blink with their own light—not us.

Also after the cosmic fuel has run out,
the finish has arrived,
all has turned to silence and stillness.

Our veins harbor the compendium of a species,
our brains—a whole universe.

And man?

The Egyptian magnificence,
The Divine Comedy,
Deep Purple *In Rock*.

How dreary to hope against hope
for a second bite at the cherry!

Doors will close on everybody's little world,
while stars will keep on blinking.

And there's no man, animal,
or any living being whatever
that can take a look beyond,
or guess, or inly know.

Someplace down below somebody's waiting on,
somewhere between now and eternity.

And if the rain should cease,
the stone would be wet all the same,
the flame would be doused all the same.

Sh ... we'd better set our minds at rest!
Sh ... just listen on ...
the perennial ticktock glides along.

Little Star

an endless night
without my little star aglow
the route is lost

Frugal Supper After Her Slamming The Door

We are here and it is now.
Further than that all human knowledge is moonshine.

HENRY LOUIS MENCKEN

The pottage is warm,
the cheese—delicious,
the water—crystalline.

Grass-scented air
inflates my lungs,
wavy skylines
ease my eyes.

A wary chaffinch
flaps and pecks
on the deal table.

Sunbeams peep
and slowly extend
on the planking
below the porch.

I'm full, fresh, amused, sedate—practiced.

I'm happy.

Year-Round Haiku

—I—

heat or chill or none
whatever is the agent
life goes on unswayed

—II—

yellow orange red
the colors of dead summer
brown will subdue soon

—III—

rainfall like a song
we hear but never follow
what the harvest tells

—IV—

through the foggy fields
alone unseen abandoned
racing to the light

—V—

he who flies from life
can hear the flaps he vibrates
makes of death his birth

—VI—

gone the languid fall
the earth returns live treasures
hues of night aglow

—VII—

eyes and hearts of ours
replete with crystal glitters
while true winter shines

—VIII—

treading on the snow
in search of vanished footprints
when the sun goes down

—IX—

days repudiate time
the elements the climate
life both dawn and dusk

—X—

green and blue advance
withdrawn the icy season
soon fresh buds will sprout

—XI—

quickly changing skies
command the vernal heyday
paint our lives anew

—XII—

sudden gusts and breaks
the way the wind is urging
all to chase their fate

—XIII—

he who botches life
can't hear the pages turning
fails to close the script

—XIV—

golden blaze by shafts
assails the parching country
killed the scent of spring

—XV—

breathless morn to eve
we long for peace and solace
deep in summertime

—XVI—

grass and bushes burned
across the torrid flatland
wells and souls run dry

—XVII—

fire or ice or none
whatever is the agent
still we have to stand

Guadeloupean Sunrise

The eastern trades—
frayed into a thousand whiffs
through the coastal palm-grove
in the south of Grande-Terre—
bring about an untimely awakening.

Neither bitter nor sweet.

Aureate spikes filter horizontally
from the thick of bananas and mangroves,
come along with a breath of unusual life.

Now everything renders it easy to understand—
how the only alternative to life is life itself.

Cradled in the slashing wail of the tropical onset.

Simply life.

Listening in the distance to the wild Atlantic
making love to the gentle Caribbean
without restraint and without respite.

Made invisible and sheltered by the sea,
yet somewhat stunned with its impossible colors
bursting at the break of day.

The ceaseless cooing of turtledoves in the ears,
the far-dazzling breakwater in the eyes,
the big marlin and Santiago surfacing from the soul.

Here and there on the opaline shoreline—
a few footprints a billion waves will never wipe off.

The Long Season

First vapor layers portend the turn—
inevitable, irreversible, impenetrable.
Banks, curtains, globes begin to haunt the land,
initially at morning and evening,
later on throughout the day.
Ever heavier fog appears in changing shapes—
the most bizarre resemble giant worms
creeping in the lactescent dusk.
The long season has just been evoked.
Now it hangs down from the sky,
sticks to men's breath,
seizes softly every object like an empty glove.
Then diamond dust will succeed.
Long watches, long musings, long silences
are waiting for those who have to wait.
As shorter days ensue through slower weeks
the long continuance spreads—
new hopes and old fancies reach out,
wrapped up in palpable unrest.
Soothing snowflakes sometimes fall and stay.
As always, time is not in haste,
the way ahead is long,
the long season is still young.
Outside a few stray cats and a solitary walker
dare its rule to clear and master the passage.

Training

Two pals.
Paths.
Fog.
Choice.

That's all that makes a day.

IN THE SAME SERIES

Published by *Troubador Publishing*

Anna Cole – *Out of the Matrix*
Francesco Agresti – *Itaca o dell'isola impossibile*
Larry Jaffe – *The Anguish of the Blacksmith's Forge*
Erminia Passannanti – *Il Roveto*
George Wallace – *Burn My Heart in Wet Sand*
Astremo/Ciofi/Lucini/Passannanti – *Poesia del dissenso: Poesia Italiana Contemporanea*
Grace Russo Bullaro – *Beyond Life is Beautiful: Comedy and Tragedy in the Cinema of Roberto Benigni*
Erminia Passannanti – *Poem of the Roses: Linguistic Expressionism in the Poems of Franco Fortini*
John Butcher and Mario Moroni (eds) – *From Eugenio Montale to Amelia Rosselli: Italian Poetry in the Sixties and Seventies*
Erminia Passannanti – *Il Corpo & Il Potere: Salò o le 120 Giornate di Sodoma di Pier Paolo Pasolini*
Gillian Ania – *Moments of Being*
Rossella Riccobono and Erminia Passannanti (eds) – *Vested Voices: Literary Transvestism in Italian Literature*

Published by *Ripostes*

Rip Bulkeley – *War Times*
Jeremy Hilton – *Slipstream*
Helen Kidd – *Ultraviolet Catastrophe*
Erminia Passannanti – *Mistici*
Ennio Abate – *Salernitudine*
Jill Haas – *The Last Days*
Brian Levison – *Adding an A*
Erminia Passannanti – *La realtà*

Review copy for Chicago Review

Printed in the United Kingdom
by Lightning Source UK Ltd.
115348UKS00001B/16-18

9 781905 237173